D1243489

GROUND ZERO

HOW A PHOTOGRAPH SENT A MESSAGE OF HOPE

by Don Nardo

Content Adviser: Thomas R. Mockaitis, PhD
Professor of History
DePaul University

COMPASS POINT BOOKS
a capstone imprint

Compass Point Books are published by Capstone,
1710 Roe Crest Drive, North Mankato, Minnesota 56003
www.mycapstone.com

Editor: Catherine Neitge
Designers: Tracy Davies McCabe and Catherine Neitge
Media Researcher: Svetlana Zhurkin
Library Consultant: Kathleen Baxter
Production Specialist: Kathy McColley

Image Credits
© 2001 North Jersey Media Group, 25, 27, 29, 33, 35, 41, 49; Alamy: Gordon
Steward, 50, Jamie Mann, 43; AP Photo: Mike Derer, 39; Department of Defense:
U.S. Marine Corps/Sgt. Don L. Maes, 21, 57; DVIC: NARA, 36; Getty Images: Photo
by 2001 *The Record* (Bergen County N.J.), cover, 15, 37, 55, 59 (right), Scott
Nelson, 19, Spencer Platt, 48, 51; Newscom: Abaca, 17, 22, 56, Reuters/Chip East,
47, Reuters/Hyungwon Kang, 23, Reuters/Kevin Lamarque, 53, 59 (left), Reuters/
Peter Morgan, 10, Reuters/STR, 5, 6, 58, UPI Photo Service/Ezio Petersen, 13;
Shutterstock: Anthony Correia, 38, Oscity, 45; Wikipedia: U.S. Air Force/Tech. Sgt.
Cedric H. Rudisill, 9, U.S. Navy/Chief Photographer's Mate Eric A. Clement, 30; XNR
Productions, 11

Library of Congress Cataloging-in-Publication Data
Cataloging-in-publication information is on file with the Library of Congress.
ISBN 978-0-7565-5425-5 (library binding)
ISBN 978-0-7565-5427-9 (paperback)
ISBN 978-0-7565-5429-3 (ebook pdf)

Printed and bound in the USA.
009691F16

TABLE**OF**CONTENTS

ChapterOne
VICTORIOUS IN SPIRIT

It was a warm and sunny morning in New York City on Tuesday, September 11, 2001. For the people of Manhattan, the regular workday had begun, and people both inside and outside of its many towering skyscrapers went about their usual tasks. Few noticed an American Airlines Boeing 767 airliner as it crossed over the nearby East River and headed for Manhattan's southern section.

At 8:46 a.m. the aircraft, carrying about 10,000 gallons (38,000 liters) of jet fuel, plowed into one of the twin towers of the World Trade Center, striking from the 93rd to the 99th floors. The impact created an enormous fireball, tore a huge hole in the North Tower's side, and instantly killed hundreds of office workers and others in the building. As a terrible fire rapidly spread within, hundreds of other people found themselves trapped in the upper stories of the 110-story building.

Soon after the collision, security officials ordered the evacuation of the north and south towers. Television stations began broadcasting live images of the burning building, alerting a shocked American public. At first many people assumed that it was a freak accident. Apparently, it seemed, a private pilot had flown his plane off-course and mistakenly

A hijacked airliner headed toward the South Tower of the World Trade Center as the North Tower burned on September 11, 2001.

struck the North Tower. It did not take long for that assumption to be proven wrong. Just 17 minutes after the aircraft hit, a second Boeing 767 bore down on the World Trade Center. It came in low over nearby buildings and smashed into the South Tower

from the 77th to the 85th floors, setting off a gigantic blast. Shards of glass and countless pieces of burning debris shot outward and showered the streets below. People now realized the awful truth. It was not an accident or a coincidence that two airliners had hit the twin towers a few minutes apart. The sequence of

The South Tower of the World Trade Center burst into flames after being hit by a hijacked airliner. The attacks killed thousands.

events could mean only one thing—the United States was under attack!

It later became known that 19 terrorists, from Saudi Arabia, the United Arab Emirates, Egypt, and Lebanon, had attacked. They belonged to a known terrorist organization, al-Qaida. Its leader was Osama bin Laden, a member of a wealthy Saudi Arabian family. The World Trade Center assault, bin Laden claimed, was retaliation for American support for such Middle Eastern Arab regimes as those in Saudi Arabia and Egypt. He considered them not true to the teachings of Islam.

As the attacks continued that morning, people stared at their television screens as one catastrophe seemed to quickly follow another. Not long after the twin towers were struck, a third airliner controlled by terrorists zeroed in on Washington, D.C. At 9:37 a.m. the plane hit the western face of the headquarters of the U.S. military, the Pentagon. The explosion destroyed much of that section of the massive concrete building, and 125 people inside were killed.

The crash also killed the 59 people on board the plane and injured more than 100 others. Terrorists flew a fourth airliner toward another target, probably the White House or U.S. Capitol, but some of the passengers fought back. The terrorists crashed the plane in a Pennsylvania field to keep the passengers from taking control. All 40 people on board died.

At about 10:00 a.m., barely a quarter of an hour after the third plane hit the Pentagon, the chaotic scene at the World Trade Center became even more deadly. The South Tower, from which immense billows of black smoke had been pouring, suddenly collapsed. Thick clouds of debris that had been pulverized by the impact expanded outward, enveloping many of the people fleeing from the site. Roughly half an hour later, the North Tower crumbled, generating more deadly debris clouds.

Nearly 3,000 people died in the World Trade Center and its vicinity. That tragic figure included more than 400 firefighters and police officers who had rushed to the scene in the minutes following the first plane's attack. More than 2,000 people were injured.

Eyewitnesses in Manhattan later recalled how they felt as the tragedy unfolded. Audrey J. Marcus, who worked at a local museum, saw the second plane hit the South Tower. "... I can remember the exact second when the whole world changed and my life changed forever. Because one minute, it was a building on fire and the next minute, none of us were safe. That's what it felt like. There was no sense of where to go, what to do, how to protect ourselves, what was going to happen next."

After the North Tower collapsed, college professor Robert Snyder said, "I look over my shoulder and now

Sections of the Pentagon were in ruins after a third deadly attack by a hijacked airliner.

Lower Manhattan is covered in apocalyptic smoke and flames. The second tower had just gone down; that was the rumble we felt. And I just looked back and saw this scene of horror to me: smoke, strange lights from flame, utterly, impossibly beautiful blue sky ultimately above it all."

As the tragedy unfolded, many people in New York City and nearby areas snapped photos and took videos of various aspects of it.

One of them was Thomas E. Franklin, a photographer for *The Record*, a northern New Jersey newspaper. He was at work in Hackensack, 5 miles (8 kilometers) from New York City. "I happened to be in the office early that day preparing for a meeting when an editor came running into the photo department saying a plane had hit the World Trade

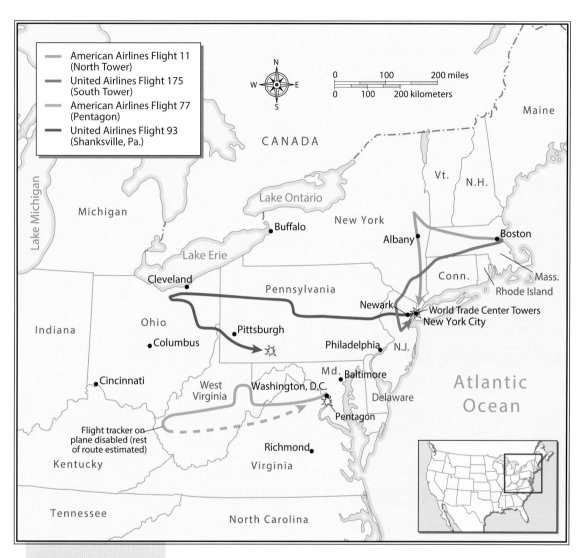

Flight paths of the four hijacked airplanes on September 11

Legend:
- American Airlines Flight 11 (North Tower)
- United Airlines Flight 175 (South Tower)
- American Airlines Flight 77 (Pentagon)
- United Airlines Flight 93 (Shanksville, Pa.)

Flight tracker on plane disabled (rest of route estimated)

Center," he said. "Immediately I knew that was no accident. Living in this area all my life, I just knew that didn't happen by chance. I ran over to the window, looked across the Meadowlands towards lower Manhattan, and saw a tremendous amount of smoke coming from the North Tower."

At first Franklin took pictures of the disaster from a distance. He had raced from the newspaper office to the Jersey City riverfront, about half a mile from the World Trade Center across the Hudson River. He was still there when the towers fell. "It was unimaginable that those two towers could come down that way," he said, "and that they were no longer there." Eventually he and a fellow photographer crossed into Manhattan by boat and worked their way toward the site of the tragedy.

When Franklin approached the smoking, twisted wreckage of what had been the World Trade Center, he found that police officers and firefighters had closed off much of the site to the public. "I walked around to the north and tried to enter from there," he later said. "I made some images over by World Trade Building 7, a tall, pinkish building on the north side of the World Trade Center Plaza." From there, he said, he shot images "of firemen dousing the smoldering wreckage, but I couldn't get into the center of Ground Zero" because it was blocked off.

As he hastily took pictures, Franklin noticed that Building 7 looked stable from the side he was standing on. But that turned out to be an illusion. "I was a mere dozen feet or so from the base of the building," he said, "but unbeknownst to me it was badly damaged on the opposite side—the Ground Zero side. I remember a fire officer then came running over to me, screaming to get out of the area. 'Get out of here!' He said, 'It's dangerous!' He then

Smoke rose from the debris of Building 7 at the World Trade Center.

had me escorted out by police and warned me not to come back, threatening arrest." Later that day Building 7 collapsed into a pile of rubble.

Despite the police barriers, not to mention the danger, Franklin managed to get past the perimeter and into the area where the two great towers had once stood. It was there, at about 5:00 p.m., that he caught sight of three firefighters unfurling an American flag. Wondering what they planned to do with it, he kept his attention riveted on them. When they raised the flag on a pole jutting upward from the rubble, he snapped several frames, including the now famous picture known as *Ground Zero Spirit*.

Franklin's newspaper sent the photo to the Associated Press, a major international news service. The image speedily circled the globe, and it came to symbolize the reality that the United States had not been permanently damaged by the 9/11 attacks.

Franklin's achievement has come to demonstrate how powerful a photograph can be to a country's citizens when they are in the midst of a national crisis. At a moment when horror and despair were widespread, the picture reminded Americans that they were far from beaten. Their strength, courage, and perseverance could and would see them through.

At a moment when horror and despair were widespread, the picture reminded Americans that they were far from beaten.

Franklin's famous photo is also known as *Raising the Flag at Ground Zero.*

ChapterTwo
PATHS TO A FATEFUL PLACE

The photo known as *Ground Zero Spirit*, taken September 11, 2001, was in part the result of one person's sudden reaction. Amid the freshly created ruins of the toppled World Trade Center towers, newspaper photographer Thomas Franklin caught sight of three firefighters raising an American flag and snapped the now iconic image. But the picture was also partly the result of the crossing of many people's paths.

Franklin followed one of those paths. His interest in photography as a young man and the location of the newspaper he ended up working for led him to that fateful place and moment in American history. Similarly, the flag raising in the rubble happened because a group of terrorists had flown planes into the World Trade Center towers hours before. The journey their organization and its leader had made in the years before the attack had been tortuous.

The leader, the founder of the terrorist group al-Qaida, was Osama bin Laden. Born into a prominent Saudi business family in 1957, he went to Afghanistan in the early 1980s. His goal was to help the Afghans, who were mainly followers of Islam, oppose the Soviets, who had invaded Afghanistan that year. They forged an anti-Soviet group of

Osama bin Laden, the leader of al-Qaida, led terrorist activities from Afghanistan.

resistance fighters known as the mujahedeen. Bin Laden became involved in the group and later took charge of bringing new fighters into Afghanistan. In the late 1980s he created a mujahedeen offshoot that in time acquired the name al-Qaida.

The Soviets suffered many casualties after their invasion and decided to abandon the operation in 1989. But many mujahedeen, bin Laden among them, chose to stay armed. They felt it was their duty to remain alert and ready to support fellow Muslims who might experience oppression in other parts of the world. The name al-Qaida means "the base" in Arabic, suggesting that it was meant to be a sort of umbrella organization for disgruntled Muslims everywhere.

In bin Laden's judgment, the 1991 U.S. invasion of Iraq was just the kind of oppression al-Qaida should resist. The goal of the operation was to force brutal Iraqi dictator Saddam Hussein to leave the tiny neighboring nation of Kuwait, which his forces had recently overrun. Bin Laden and other al-Qaida members despised Saddam and agreed that he had to be evicted from Kuwait. But they were staunchly opposed to the Saudi policy of allowing U.S. soldiers to use Saudi Arabian territory to launch assaults on Saddam. In bin Laden's view, Americans and other westerners were infidels—non-followers of the Islamic faith. It was therefore an insult to God to allow such fighters to occupy Saudi Arabian soil, which all Muslims saw as holy.

True to that belief, bin Laden spoke out against Saudi Arabia's pro-western stance. Saudi leaders claimed he did not speak for them, promptly revoked his citizenship, and banished him from the country. These events convinced bin Laden and his top al-Qaida associates that the United States and other

The American presence in the Middle East angered bin Laden and his followers.

western nations, working with the Saudis, were out to control Muslim countries.

At first Al-Qaida's leaders, including Osama bin Laden and his future second in command, Ayman al-Zawahiri, chose the Sudan, an African nation, as a base of operations. But in 1996 increasing pressure from the United States persuaded Sudanese officials to expel bin Laden and his organization. Al-Qaida then set up shop in Afghanistan, which was ruled by a group of Muslim extremists known as the Taliban. There, in secluded training camps, al-Qaida prepared its growing ranks of fighters to wage war against the West.

Bin Laden and Zawahiri did not try to conceal their hatred for the West, especially the United States, and their desire to harm western nations. For example, in February 1998 the two men issued an Islamic legal decree called a fatwa, even though neither was a religious leader with the authority to do so. The decree said in part that it was the duty of all Muslims to kill Americans and their allies— both soldiers and civilians—whenever possible. "By God's leave," the fatwa stated, "we call on every Muslim who believes in God and hopes for reward to obey God's command to kill the Americans and plunder their possessions wherever he finds them and whenever he can."

Al-Qaida soon began its vendetta against the West, secretly sending agents armed with bombs to East Africa. On August 7, 1998, the bombs exploded at the U.S. embassies in Kenya and Tanzania, killing 224 people and wounding more than 5,000. Two years later terrorists working for al-Qaida severely damaged an American warship, the USS *Cole*, while it was refueling in Yemen, on the southern tip of the Arabian Peninsula. Seventeen U.S. sailors lost their lives, and 39 more were injured.

Americans and other westerners were shocked by the ruthless attacks and strongly condemned them. Yet most Americans still felt relatively safe. After all, the bombings of the embassies and the *Cole* had

The USS *Cole* was heavily damaged and 17 sailors were killed in a terrorist attack in 2000.

occurred in places that were far from the United States. So very few Americans could imagine a major assault by al-Qaida, or any other terrorist group, on U.S. soil.

That horrifying scenario became real on September 11, 2001. Under the orders of bin Laden and other al-Qaida commanders, 19 terrorists planned and trained carefully for attacks on important symbols of the U.S. government and economy. Bin Laden and Zawahiri targeted the Pentagon, the heart of U.S. military strategy and

Ayman al-Zawahiri, an Egyptian doctor, would eventually become the leader of al-Qaida.

planning, and the World Trade Center in Manhattan, a chief emblem of big business. Other probable targets were the U.S. Capitol, where Congress meets and makes laws, or the White House, the residence of the American president. The al-Qaida planners appeared to think that such destruction would prompt the United States to invade Afghanistan and become hopelessly bogged down there. That, they apparently believed, would persuade Americans and their allies to stop meddling in Middle Eastern affairs.

Bin Laden had planned carefully. And although

The Washington Monument loomed behind the Pentagon, which was heavily damaged on September 11.

not all aspects of the operation worked, it still did tremendous damage. The 19 attackers successfully hijacked four commercial airliners loaded with passengers and used them as weapons by crashing three of them into the Pentagon and the north and south towers of the World Trade Center. It has been estimated that the terrorist operation cost $500,000, but it inflicted more than $3 trillion in damages on the United States.

Across the Hudson River from the World Trade Center, photographer Thomas Franklin could see the smoke pouring from the North Tower. But he knew that to cover the story best he needed to be much closer to the action.

"The bridges and tunnels into the city were now shut down," he later said, "so I continued driving south towards Jersey City. I must have been doing 90 mph at this point. I made it to Exchange Place, a financial district with tall buildings and a bustling downtown located on the Jersey City riverfront. As the crow flies it's maybe a half a mile from the World Trade, just across the Hudson River. It's also a ferry port for commuters. Short of getting into New York, it was about the best location for shooting what was happening. That's where I made pictures all morning."

Franklin knew that documenting a major historical event was a vital service, not only to his newspaper but also to society and future generations. "I knew what I was doing was important," he later said, "but I didn't want to become emotionally impaired either. Clearly I was documenting history, that was foremost in my mind. In a way, working the story and photographing kept my mind from wondering about the personal connections and the long-term ramifications of what was happening."

Along the Jersey docks, Franklin saw thousands of people arriving by boat from Manhattan, some of whom were wounded. Most of the evacuees were

The injured were rushed to New Jersey hospitals after being evacuated from Manhattan by boat.

covered with dust. Health-care providers had set up a triage center near the shore, and ambulances hurriedly came and went. "You had all of this happening with the backdrop of the New York City skyline billowing smoke," Franklin said. "It was very dramatic."

About 1:00 p.m. Franklin fell in with John Wheeler, another photographer documenting the historic event. The two men managed to board a tugboat headed across the river, and about half an hour later they were approaching the 47-story building known as World Trade Center 7. Although Franklin tried to get closer to Ground Zero several times, the police threatened to arrest him if he did not stay back. But the photographer knew he had to get to Ground Zero.

One thing that hampered him was the scale of the destruction. "The wreckage was so vast," Franklin said, "it was hard to focus on any one thing, or to capture the scope of it all. I remembered making pictures of mounds of smoldering metal piled high. Everything was gray, there was no color, the landscape was unrecognizable. Everyone I saw was in shock. It looked like a battle scene from a movie, smoke and dust everywhere."

Other people who stood near Ground Zero agreed. "I took a deep breath of dusty, smoke-filled, soot-filled air," said Scott P. Strauss, a police officer working with an emergency service unit, "and then I heard myself say, 'I love you,' to my wife and my kids, and I started to crawl into the hole. I didn't think I was ever coming out of there.

"We had to crawl down on an angle about 20 feet, maybe a little further, over twisted steel, around

"The wreckage was so vast, it was hard to focus on any one thing, or to capture the scope of it all."

Franklin captured firefighters working above the rubble at Ground Zero.

concrete slabs, and over just piles of rubble. I hit a wall, turned to the left, went about 10 feet to the left, again around stuff, over stuff, and there was what was left of an elevator shaft that went down—how many levels, I don't know."

As Franklin painstakingly made his way through the rubble, he lost track of time. About 5:00 p.m. he saw the three firefighters with whom he would thereafter be forever linked. They were "about 100 feet away, standing up on a rise," he later remembered. "I saw them doing something with an American flag."

Franklin later explained what happened next. "I made the picture standing underneath what may have been one of the elevated walkways, possibly the one that had connected the World Trade Plaza and the World Financial Center. As soon as I shot it," he said, "I realized the similarity to the famous image of Marines raising the flag at Iwo Jima," a Pulitzer Prize-winning photo taken during World War II.

"This was an important shot," Franklin said. "It told more than just death and destruction. It said something to me about the strength of the American people and of these firemen having to battle the unimaginable."

In the photographer's reconstruction of the event, he snapped the shutter, creating the iconic image, at 5:01 p.m. from a distance of about 30 yards (27 meters). "I saw the firemen with the flag, and a flagpole wedged at an odd angle atop a pile of rubble about 15 feet high," he said. "I waited, unsure what was happening. Just then the fireman in the center, Dan McWilliams, hoisted the flag up the pole. His colleagues, George Johnson and Billy Eisengrein,

Three firefighters shortly after raising the flag at Ground Zero

looked on. I pointed my camera and shot a burst of frames as the flag went up."

It all happened very quickly and without any drama or fanfare. "I don't think they had any idea that their spontaneous act of patriotism was being photographed," Franklin said.

Then Franklin felt it was time to leave and get the shots he had made that day to his editors. They would decide what to use in the newspaper's next issue. He had to get back across the river to New Jersey by boat and then walk to his car. When he got off the boat,

FAMOUS FLAG IS MISSING

What was thought to be the Ground Zero flag was presented to the crew of the USS Theodore Roosevelt *on September 30, 2001.*

Where did the famous flag come from, and where is it now? The answer to the first question is easy. The answer to the second question? Who knows?

Dan McWilliams of Brooklyn Ladder Company 157 spotted the flag on a yacht docked a few hundred feet from the ruins of the World Trade Center. The *Star of America*, owned by a Greek-American couple, Spiro Kopelakis and Shirley Dreifus, was flying a flag made by Eder Flag Manufacturing of Oak Creek, Wisconsin. After the two towers collapsed, it struck McWilliams that the dedicated but distraught rescue workers could use some extra patriotic encouragement, and he took the flag to display in the ruins. Soon he and his colleagues George Johnson, also of Ladder 157,

and Billy Eisengrein, of Brooklyn Rescue Company Two, raised the flag, and Thomas Franklin snapped his iconic photo.

A few weeks later, a flag was raised at Yankee Stadium in front of 20,000 people who had gathered to remember the victims of the September 11 attacks. It was then given to the Navy to fly on ships heading to fight terrorists in Afghanistan. It returned to New York City in 2002 after its travels. But it wasn't the real flag. It was an impostor. The real flag had disappeared—possibly within hours of its raising. The flag's owners want to give the flag to a museum. But first they have to find it.

ready to walk the few miles to his car, he noticed that the police had set up a decontamination center in his path. They were hosing down people who were covered with dust and grime. "I said to myself, 'No way I'm going through that,'" Franklin said. "I needed to make deadline and I didn't have time for this. So I made a run for it, like in *The Fugitive*. I bolted from the line and ran across an open field towards the parking lot, sprinting all the way."

After the photo of the flag-raising became popular, people mused about the far-flung, complex, and unlikely circumstances that had converged to allow the image to be created. Al-Qaida's leaders, along with the 19 hijackers, had followed their individual, twisting paths to that momentous day. So had Franklin. And so had the three firefighters who had bravely responded to the tragedy and thoughtfully taken the time to hoist the flag.

When all the threads had been woven together, Franklin's photo foreshadowed America's rise from the ashes of 9/11. "Of all the pictures from the day of pictures, this was the one that presented a semblance of hope," wrote David Friend in his book *Watching the World Change: The Stories Behind the Images of 9/11*. "Standing on the mount where thousands had been killed, three men had thought to raise a flag 'caked in crud,' as one of them would put it, to rally the living and honor the dead."

ChapterThree
ANALYZING AN ICONIC IMAGE

It was no accident that Thomas Franklin's photo of the flag-raising at Ground Zero became so popular with Americans in the aftermath of the 9/11 attacks. Experts on photography, journalists, and casual observers alike agree that it is an extremely powerful visual image. In large part, that is because its considerable complexity is belied by its apparent simplicity.

At first Franklin's picture seems to be a straightforward, uncomplicated shot of three men hoisting a flag. Yet on a deeper level, the image contains a large amount of information. Various less apparent elements of the shot appeal to various types of viewers in emotional, cultural, and other ways. "Tom's image—its succinctness and its compression of information in a small place—gives it an iconic nature," said author David Friend, a former photo editor at *Life* magazine.

In retrospect, neither Franklin nor the three firefighters he captured on film—Dan McWilliams, George Johnson, and Billy Eisengrein—had any notion at that moment that they were creating something iconic. All four men were caught up in the drama and raw emotions of a frightening national tragedy. How could they have known that what they

A firefighter searched for survivors in one of the many photos taken at Ground Zero.

were doing would touch a nerve with millions of people for years afterward?

The immediate events on September 11 that led

to the taking of the photo began a little after 4:30 in the afternoon. The three Brooklyn firefighters were searching for survivors in the rubble of the fallen towers. McWilliams saw an American flag on a yacht docked nearby and retrieved it. With the help of Johnson and Eisengrein, he raised the flag on a pole they found in the rubble. At that moment, completely by chance, Franklin, carrying his camera, happened by and captured the event for posterity.

Franklin explained that he had positioned himself and "a moment later I see the flag going up. I shot a quick burst of frames. Then it was over. There was no performance, they didn't do it for an audience. No words were exchanged."

"The question everyone asks," he said, "is 'Did you know what you had?' The answer is—no way. At the time, it didn't stand out to me. Three men raising a flag did not seem very important to me at that time. Two of the largest, most recognizable buildings in the world came crashing down on thousands of innocent people. What happened seemed apocalyptic. So how could this act even compare?"

Not long after taking the shot, however, Franklin realized that it was similar in several ways to a very famous picture from World War II. Photographer Joe Rosenthal, then with the Associated Press, had snapped an image of a group of U.S. Marines raising the American flag on the South Pacific island of

"There was no performance, they didn't do it for an audience. No words were exchanged."

Franklin photographed the famous flag after the firefighters left the scene.

Iwo Jima after one of the conflict's bloodiest battles. "It momentarily dawned on me," said Franklin, that the picture of the firefighters raising the flag partly resembled Rosenthal's image. "But in no way was it [purposely] constructed that way. It happened more like a play in sports—you have a brief moment or two

to size it up, position yourself, compose it, zoom in or out, and press the shutter."

One difference between the two iconic photos is that Rosenthal did not live and work in the digital age. Only a handful of images were snapped of the 1945 victory at Iwo Jima, in part because very few

Joe Rosenthal's photograph of the flag-raising at Iwo Jima became an icon of bravery and hope during wartime.

Franklin's powerful image became a symbol of hope more than 65 years after another iconic photo was taken during World War II.

people there had cameras. So the American public ended up seeing only Rosenthal's picture repeatedly. It became a distinctive piece of historical evidence documenting the Iwo Jima victory.

Devices that create instant digital images are everywhere today. So when a major event, like a

national disaster, takes place, the public is barraged
with hundreds or even thousands of photos taken
by professional photographers and ordinary people
alike. Tens of thousands of still photos and videos
were taken September 11. What makes certain
images among so many more memorable than others
and more valuable as historical evidence?

Franklin had to deal with that question when
examining his own photos. He faced the daunting
task of deciding which of the images he would share
with the public and with posterity.

MIXED FEELINGS ABOUT PHOTO

Thomas Franklin calls Ground Zero Spirit *the most meaningful photo he has ever taken.*

Despite the many evaluations of Thomas Franklin's photo of the flag-raising, he maintains his own, at times mixed, feelings about its quality and importance. He expressed his thoughts in a December 2011 interview, a little more than a decade after he took the picture.

"That day and for the next few months it became a balancing act of trying to do my job while trying to accommodate the requests for the picture and my time. It was stressful, and it became bittersweet because the image was receiving a lot of attention, yet at the same time there were thousands of people dead—hundreds in our readership area alone. It was an emotional time," he said.

"There was an immense sense of loss, a sense of loss that lasted for a long, long time, and still exists for many. Very early I separated myself from it. It wasn't about me, it has always been about the relationship people have with the picture. Photography is so much about the feeling people get from looking at an image.

"To me, this picture is about thousands of innocent people who were murdered and died in the most horrific way imaginable. Innocent people, who died senselessly. Any discussion about 9/11 has to be about that first and foremost. I believe that.

"I don't feel defined by this picture, I'm not sure it's the best picture I've ever made. I don't even know if it's the best picture of that day. But clearly it's the most meaningful picture I've made," he said.

When he made it back to New Jersey after nightfall, he had not yet decided which of the many images were more visually effective or more newsworthy than others. He sent 31 images to the newspaper, including the flag-raising photo. It "didn't stand out to me," he said later, "it was one of the last pictures I moved."

A short time later, Franklin received a phone call from the paper's photo editor, Rich Gigli, about the flag-raising image. "What's going on here?" Gigli asked. "I told him they were raising the flag, and it happened very quickly." The photographer added that he had few details about the incident and wanted to know what Gigli thought about some of the other photos he had taken. But Gigli kept bringing the conversation back to the image of the firefighters and the flag. "We really think it's very strong," he told Franklin.

The excellent visual composition of the photo is worthy of special note. The underlying geometric shapes give the image a strong sense of balance. "The flagpole cuts across the frame," an article in *The Record* noted on the 10-year anniversary of the attacks, "with the flag unfurling in the center and the figures below, to give the photo an elemental, triangular structure. The late afternoon light catches the bright colors of the flag and uniforms, giving them a sculptural quality against the ash-covered background."

Franklin captured two stunned firefighters overcome with emotion at Ground Zero.

Viewers have also remarked on the photo's powerful emotional content. Any photo has emotional qualities when viewers perceive that it has a point of view that touches them on an emotional level. In this case the chief viewers were Americans. Although they regularly disagree on a great many topics, history has shown that Americans tend to come together quickly when the country is under attack. The photo promotes such a sense of unity.

Another emotional response that Franklin's

photo draws from its American audience is a shared feeling of patriotism. Franklin said one of the reasons his image "resonated with so many was because it was viewed largely as a symbol of patriotism, pride and strength. A seemingly positive image, on a day where nearly every other image made pictured death and destruction."

From feelings of loyalty to the nation, it is only a short step to sharing American values. That too is part of the information inherent in Franklin's iconic photo. Scholar Meg Spratt, co-author of a study of familiar images of the American flag, explained that with iconic photos, "visual images have the potential to elicit shared emotional reactions and at times even the impetus to political action" by people who read or watch the daily news.

Visual images containing strong emotional content, like Franklin's photo, help to shape people's memories of important events. Years after such an event, mention of it often conjures a vision of an iconic photo taken at the time, even if most details of the event have been forgotten. Rosenthal's image of the Marines raising the flag on Iwo Jima is an example. Despite the passage of more than 70 years, many people who hear or read "Iwo Jima" immediately see that image in their mind's eye. Similarly, for many people, Franklin's photo comes to mind when they hear or read "World Trade Center" or "9/11."

Front pages of newspapers on September 12, 2001, reflected the horror of the attacks.

Franklin's photo also makes a statement related to time. The image not only speaks to viewers about the attack and Americans' mutual emotions, values, and ideals, but it also considers what might happen next at Ground Zero. According to Guy Westwell, a London-based expert on movies, photography, and culture, "The upwards direction of the firefighters' gazes and their work to raise the flag pulls the viewer's focus into the sky above, registering both the space left empty by the collapse of the twin towers but also a sense of what might come to fill this space. In temporal terms—and keenly felt by those monitoring the event on television and in newspapers on 12 September—the normality of 10 September is tied to the acute memory of September 11, and then to a sense of trepidation about the future."

Franklin's famous photo did raise the question of what might fill the space left by the destroyed twin towers. That question was answered with finality 13 years later. A new skyscraper opened November 3, 2014, on the spot where the original towers had stood. Known as One World Trade Center, it stands a symbolic 1,776 feet (541 meters) tall. That number—corresponding to 1776, the year of U.S. independence—appeals to the same sense of shared patriotism that Franklin's picture of the 2001 flag-raising does.

So in a very real way, the iconic photo—*Ground Zero Spirit*—indirectly peered into the future. The image, which displays the ruins of two great structures, hints at the coming of an even more imposing building—the tallest in the Western Hemisphere. Some observers have even seen the flag raised by the three firefighters as symbolic of the poking up of a new plant's first tiny shoot from the barren rubble. Over time, they say, that fresh emblem of the unbreakable American spirit would steadily reach for the sky and eventually, as One World Trade Center, tower over a still proud people.

One World Trade Center dominates the skyline of Lower Manhattan.

ChapterFour
ONGOING LEGACY

Thomas Franklin's *Ground Zero Spirit* reached the public in the September 12, 2001, issue of *The Record* and many other newspapers. The photo was instantly popular. That night the firefighters in the picture began hearing congratulations from their families and friends. The men were at first surprised, since until then they hadn't known that their spontaneous flag-raising had been photographed.

But this was only the start of the attention the men would receive. Within a few days, McWilliams, Johnson, and Eisengrein started to get calls from television and radio programs asking them to appear on talk shows. They rarely spoke to the press. Meanwhile, *The Record* was bombarded with requests for reprints of the image—more than 30,000 in all. Businesses reprinted the photo on T-shirts, pins, hats, cereal boxes, children's lunch boxes, and other products.

Interest in the picture did not let up, and artistic reproductions became common. Barbershops, hair salons, bars, bus stations, auto repair shops, and business offices hung copies, while more creative versions appeared as well. One memorable example was a mural of the flag-raising painted by a prison inmate in New Orleans, Louisiana.

A lifelike wax re-creation of Franklin's iconic photo is on display at Madame Tussauds, a wax museum in New York City.

Franklin saw a two-story-high adaptation painted on the side of a building in New York City. He later recalled many other commercial and artistic

A New York City fire truck features a mural based on the famous flag-raising photograph.

examples. "People used to send me stuff," he said. "I mean crazy stuff. Clocks, wristwatches, seat covers, chocolate bars, pumpkin carvings! Friends still send me pictures when they see it in strange places. I have quite a collection."

FOREVER LINKED

The firefighters in the iconic photo have shunned the spotlight and rarely give interviews. They want to maintain their privacy, in part, they say, because the photo has been compared to the famous picture of the flag-raising at Iwo Jima. Billy Eisengrein pointed out that few Americans can name the Marines in the famous World War II photo.

"We're pretty adamant about not letting that change who we are and what we are," he told ABC News on the 10th anniversary of the attacks. "Let the picture stand for itself."

The three firefighters, Eisengrein, Dan McWilliams, and George Johnson, used money they earned from licensing the photo to establish The Bravest Fund, a charity to help emergency workers and others affected by the attacks. Thousands of workers suffered health problems after inhaling the dust and debris at the attack site. The firefighters have given away more than $1 million to help pay medical bills, Eisengrein said. "We've helped a lot of firefighters' families, a number of construction workers, and a few other people."

He said people have told him many times that the picture helped them understand that "we as a country, we're going to be OK. The three of us are very proud ... and honored to have been a part of that."

The firefighters walked away after raising the flag caught in the iconic photo.

A Louisiana fire department building bears a mural based on the famous image.

Several artistic renditions of the photo took minor liberties with its form and composition, but most of those raised little or no controversy. One major exception was a proposed sculpture based directly on Franklin's photo. Intended as a tribute to the 343 firefighters who died on 9/11, it was commissioned by the New York Fire Department. A clay model of the statue was unveiled late in 2001. It raised eyebrows because it portrayed one of the firefighters as white, another black, and the third Latino.

The controversy was based on the fact that McWilliams, Johnson, and Eisengrein are white.

A clay model of a proposed sculpture based on Franklin's photo was unveiled amid controversy.

Some people felt offended by the change, and they accused the artist of trying to rewrite history to be politically correct. Yet, as Frank Gribbon, a spokesman for the New York City Fire Department, pointed out, the specific firefighters who raised the flag were not the men being honored. The idea was to honor all New York City firefighters who had died. "Given that those who died were of all races and all ethnicities," he said, "and that the statue was to be symbolic of those sacrifices, ultimately a decision was made to honor no one in particular, but everyone who made the supreme sacrifice." As a result of continuing disagreements over the project, it was eventually scrapped.

Franklin's *Ground Zero Spirit* received many recognitions and honors. Late in 2001 the Associated Press Media Editors group chose it as the "showcase photo of the year." It was named photo of the year by *Editor & Publisher* magazine. *Life* magazine called it one of the "100 photos that changed the world." The picture was a finalist for the prestigious Pulitzer Prize. Although it did not win—*The New York Times* won for a portfolio of 20 photos of the attack and its aftermath—Franklin felt that just to be a finalist was a tremendous honor.

The U.S. Postal Service issued a stamp bearing the image of the three firefighters raising the flag. President George W. Bush unveiled the stamp at a ceremony in March 2002 that was attended by Franklin and the three firefighters. Although first-class stamps then cost 34 cents, the one featuring *Ground Zero Spirit* sold for 45 cents. The $10.5 million raised through the extra 11 cents went

Life magazine called it one of the "100 photos that changed the world."

The three firefighters stood with President George W. Bush as a stamp based on their photo was unveiled in 2002.

to the Federal Emergency Management Agency, which gave it to families of rescuers killed or disabled in the terrorist attacks. The stamp was sold for about two years.

Franklin remains humble about the photo. He has frequently said that it was merely a coincidence, or an accident, that he happened upon the flag-raising. He has also argued that he was just doing his job that day and trying to meet his newspaper's deadline under unusually difficult circumstances.

At the same time, Franklin realizes the significance of what he did. Although he thinks blind chance placed him where he was at the right time, he recognizes that the photo struck a major nerve with Americans. "I still get letters, phone calls, and emails about it," he said, many years after 9/11. "To me, that speaks volumes of the power of a picture. And this picture has lived a life of its own. It went viral, and it was used in a way that did a lot of good. That's pretty cool.

"I don't spend a lot of time thinking about it though, or dwelling on it. I think I did great work before then, and I've certainly done some great work since then. In many ways it seems like a long time ago."

Like a true professional, Franklin sees his iconic photo not as his main legacy but rather just part of his entire body of work. "I don't think making the picture has changed me at all," he said. "I just always try to be true to myself. I think as a photojournalist you let the pictures do the talking. I just try to stick with that."

Ground Zero Spirit captured the moment when three firefighters raised the American flag as a symbol of hope and freedom.

Timeline

1988

Osama bin Laden, mastermind of the 9/11 attacks, establishes a terrorist group he names al-Qaida

1993

Thomas E. Franklin begins working as a photographer at *The Record*, in Bergen County, New Jersey

1998

Bin Laden issues an Islamic decree called a fatwa against western nations, and al-Qaida attacks some of their embassies

1996

Bin Laden and his al-Qaida associates are expelled from Sudan, in Africa, and move their operations to Afghanistan

October 12, 2000

Al-Qaida terrorists heavily damage an American warship, the USS *Cole*, in Yemen

Timeline

SEPTEMBER 11, 2001

8:46 a.m.

An airliner piloted by a member of al-Qaida strikes the World Trade Center's North Tower; it collapses at 10:28 a.m.

9:03 a.m.

A second airliner hits the World Trade Center's South Tower; it collapses at 9:59 a.m.

September 12, 2001

The Record and other newspapers print Franklin's iconic photo, *Ground Zero Spirit*

9:37 a.m.

A third plane hijacked by al-Qaida crashes into the Pentagon, in Washington, D.C.

10:03 a.m.

A fourth plane hijacked by al-Qaida crashes into a field near Shanksville, Pennsylvania, after passengers counterattack

About 5:00 p.m.

Franklin sees three firefighters raising the American flag amid the rubble and captures the event with his camera

March 11, 2002

President George W. Bush unveils a postage stamp bearing the image of the *Ground Zero Spirit* photo

May 2, 2011

U.S. Special Operations forces kill Osama bin Laden at his home in Pakistan

Glossary

apocalyptic—involving the most severe destruction imaginable

accommodate—to make room for

fatwa—legal opinion or decree handed down by an Islamic religious leader

iconic—widely viewed as perfectly capturing the meaning or spirit of something or someone

Islam—religion founded on the Arabian Peninsula in the seventh century by the prophet Muhammad; the religion's followers are called Muslims

mujahedeen—Islamic guerrilla fighters, especially in the Middle East

perseverance—the act of continually trying or committing to a certain action or belief

posterity—future ages and generations

regime—the government in power

spontaneous—without previous thought or planning

succinct—characterized by brief and precise expression

temporal—relating to time

trepidation—feeling of fear about something that may happen

triage center—place where victims are sorted based on the urgency of their needs

vendetta—long bitter quarrel with or campaign against someone

Additional Resources

Further Reading

Benoit, Peter. *September 11 Then and Now*.
New York: Children's Press, 2012.

Brown, Don. *America Is Under Attack: September 11, 2001: The Day the Towers Fell*.
New York: Roaring Brook Press, 2011.

Hampton, Wilborn. *September 11, 2001; Attack on New York City*. Cambridge, Mass.: Candlewick, 2011.

Thoms, Annie, ed. *With their Eyes: September 11th, The View from a High School at Ground Zero*.
New York: HarperTempest, 2011.

Internet Sites

Use FactHound to find Internet sites related to this book. All of the sites on FactHound have been researched by our staff.

Here's all you do:
Visit *www.facthound.com*
Type in this code: 9780756554255

Critical Thinking Using the Common Core

Why did Osama bin Laden despise and target various western nations, especially the United States? Rather than resorting to violence and mass murder, what would have been a better approach for him to take in airing his grievances? (Integration of Knowledge and Ideas)

The three firefighters pictured in *Ground Zero Spirit* received money from licensing products bearing their images. Do you approve of how they used the funds? (Key Ideas and Details)

What factors contribute to the lasting power and appeal of Thomas Franklin's iconic photo? (Craft and Structure)

Source Notes

Page 8, line 20: "Witness to Apocalypse." Columbia Center for Oral History. 8 Sept. 2011. 17 Feb. 2016. *The New York Times*. http://www.nytimes.com/2011/09/08/us/sept-11-reckoning/escape.html?_r=0

Page 8, line 28: Ibid.

Page 10, line 7: "Spotlight on Thomas Franklin." The Image, Deconstructed. 16 Dec. 2011. 16 May 2016. http://imagedeconstructed.com/post/spotlight-on-thomas-franklin/

Page 12, line 3: Ibid.

Page 12, line 12: Ibid.

Page 12, line 23: Ibid.

Page 20, line 9: Frank A. Biggio. "Neutralizing the Threat: Reconsidering Existing Doctrines in the Emerging War on Terrorism." *Case Western Reserve Journal of International Law*. Volume 34, Issue 1, 2002. 18 Feb. 2016. http://scholarlycommons.law.case.edu/cgi/viewcontent.cgi?article=1443&context=jil

Page 24, line 4: "Spotlight on Thomas Franklin."

Page 24, line 19: Ibid.

Page 25, line 3: Ibid.

Page 26, line 12: Ibid.

Page 26, line 21: "Witness to Apocalypse."

Page 28, line 5: "Spotlight on Thomas Franklin."

Page 28, line 9: Kenneth Irby. "One Man's Path to Historic Photo: Persistence and a Lift on a Tug." Poynter. 2 Sept. 2002. 16 May 2016. http://www.poynter.org/2002/one-mans-path-to-historic-photo-persistence-and-a-lift-on-a-tug/2302/

Page 28, line 16: Derek Rubin and Jaap Verheul, eds. *American Multiculturalism After 9/11: Transatlantic Perspectives*. Amsterdam: Amsterdam University Press, 2009, p. 113

Page 28, line 24: Lindy Washburn. "Flag image presented a 'semblance of hope' on 9/11." *The Record*. 6 Sept. 2011. 18 Feb. 2016. http://www.northjersey.com/news/flag-image-presented-a-semblance-of-hope-on-9-11-1.320385

Page 31, line 4: "Spotlight on Thomas Franklin."

Page 31, line 21: David Friend. *Watching the World Change: The Stories Behind the Images of 9/11*. New York: Farrar, Straus, and Giroux, 2006, p. 311

Page 32, line 15: "Flag image presented a 'semblance of hope' on 9/11."

Page 34, line 11: "Spotlight on Thomas Franklin."

Page 35, line 2: Ibid.

Page 39, line 6: Ibid

Page 40, line 5: Ibid.

Page 40, line 10: Ibid.

Page 40, line 22: "Flag image presented a 'semblance of hope' on 9/11."

Page 42, line 3: "Spotlight on Thomas Franklin."

Page 42, line 13: Meg Spratt, April Peterson and Taso Lagos. "Of Photographs and Flags: Uses and Perceptions of an Iconic Image Before and After September 11, 2001." *Popular Communication*, Volume 3, Issue 2, 2005, p. 120.

Page 43, line 7: Guy Westwell. "One image begets another: a comparative analysis of Flag-Raising on Iwo Jima and Ground Zero Spirit." *Journal of War and Culture Studies*, Volume 1, Number 3, 2008, p. 329.

Page 48, line 1: "Spotlight on Thomas Franklin."

Page 49, lines 11, 28: Christina Caron. "9/11 Firefighter Speaks With ABC News 10 Years Later." 7 Sept. 2011. 17 Feb. 2016. ABC News. http://abcnews.go.com/US/September_11/911-firefighter-speaks-abc-news-10-years/story?id=14456184

Page 52, line 4: The Associated Press. "Statue of trade center flag-raising rebuked." *The Baltimore Sun*. 12 Jan. 2002. 16 May 2016. http://www.baltimoresun.com/bal-te.statue12jan12-story.html

Page 54, line 3: "Spotlight on Thomas Franklin."

Page 54, line 16: Ibid.

Select Bibliography

The Associated Press. "Statue of trade center flag-raising rebuked." *The Baltimore Sun*. 12 Jan. 2002. 18 Feb. 2016. http://www.baltimoresun.com/bal-te.statue12jan12-story. html

Biggio, Frank A. "Neutralizing the Threat: Reconsidering Existing Doctrines in the Emerging War on Terrorism." *Case Western Reserve Journal of International Law*. Volume 34, Issue 1, 2002. 18 Feb. 2016. http://scholarlycommons.law.case.edu/cgi/viewcontent.cgi?article=1443&context=jil

Bin Laden, Osama. Bruce Lawrence, ed. *Messages to the World: The Statements of Osama Bin Laden*. New York: Verso, 2005.

Caron, Christina. "9/11 Firefighter Speaks With ABC News 10 Years Later." ABC News. 7 Sept. 2011. 17 Feb. 2016. http://abcnews.go.com/US/September_11/911-firefighter-speaks-abc-news-10-years/story?id=14456184

Ehrenberg, John, ed. *The Iraq Papers*. New York: Oxford University Press, 2010.

Friend, David. *Watching the World Change: The Stories Behind the Images of 9/11*. New York: Farrar, Straus, and Giroux, 2006.

Ground Zero Spirit. North Jersey Media Group Foundation. 19 May 2016. http://www.groundzerospirit.org/about.asp

Hampson, Rick. "The photo no one will forget." *USA Today*. 27 Dec. 2001. 18 Feb. 2016. http://usatoday30.usatoday.com/news/sept11/2001/12/27/usatcov-unforgettable.htm

Haught, James A. *Holy Horrors: An Illustrated History of Religious Murder and Madness*. Buffalo, N.Y.: Prometheus Books, 1990.

Help Find the Flag. 16 May 2016. http://www.findthe911flag.com/

Irby, Kenneth. "One Man's Path to Historic Photo: Persistence and a Lift on a Tug." Poynter. 2 Sept. 2002. 18 Feb. 2016. http://www.poynter.org/2002/one-mans-path-to-historic-photo-persistence-and-a-lift-on-a-tug/2302/

Johnson, Joel, Matt Buchanan, and Scott Alexander. "9/11: The Photographers' Stories, Pt.1—'Get Down Here. Now.'" *American Photo*. 7 Sept. 2011. 17 Feb. 2016. http://www.americanphotomag.com/91101-photographers-stories-pt-1-get-down-here-now

Leffler, Melvyn P. "September 11 in Retrospect: George W. Bush's Grand Strategy, Reconsidered." *Foreign Affairs*. September/October 2011. 17 Feb. 2016. https://www.foreignaffairs.com/articles/2011-08-19/september-11-retrospect

Mahan, Sue, and Pamala L. Griset. *Terrorism in Perspective*. Thousand Oaks, Calif.: Sage Publications, 2013.

Mockaitis, Thomas R. *Osama bin Laden: A Biography*. Santa Barbara, Calif.: Greenwood, 2010.

One Nation: America Remembers September 11, 2001: 10 Years Later. New York: Little, Brown and Company, 2011.

Rubin, Derek, and Jaap Verheul, eds. *American Multiculturalism After 9/11: Transatlantic Perspectives*. Amsterdam: Amsterdam University Press, 2009.

Simmons, Anthony, and Robbyn Swan. *The Eleventh Day: The Full Story of 9/11 and Osama bin Laden*. New York: Ballantine Books, 2012.

"Spotlight on Thomas Franklin." The Image, Deconstructed. 16 Dec. 2011. 17 Feb. 2016. http://imagedeconstructed.com/post/spotlight-on-thomas-franklin/

Spratt, Meg, April Peterson and Taso Lagos. "Of Photographs and Flags: Uses and Perceptions of an Iconic Image Before and After September 11, 2001." *Popular Communication*, Volume 3, Issue 2, 2005.

Sweet, Christopher, ed. *Above Hallowed Ground: A Photographic Record of September 11, 2001*. New York: Viking Studio, 2002.

Timeline: Osama bin Laden, over the years. CNN.com. 2 May 2011. 18 Feb. 2016. http://www.cnn.com/2011/WORLD/asiapcf/05/02/bin.laden.timeline/

Washburn, Lindy. "Flag image presented a 'semblance of hope' on 9/11." *The Record*. 6 Sept. 2011. 18 Feb. 2016. http://www.northjersey.com/news/flag-image-presented-a-semblance-of-hope-on-9-11-1.320385

Westwell, Guy. "One image begets another: a comparative analysis of Flag-Raising on Iwo Jima and Ground Zero Spirit." *Journal of War and Culture Studies*, Volume 1, Number 3, 2008.

"Witness to Apocalypse." Columbia Center for Oral History. 8 Sept. 2011. 17 Feb. 2016. *The New York Times*. http://www.nytimes.com/2011/09/08/us/sept-11-reckoning/escape.html?_r=0

Wright, Lawrence. *The Looming Tower: Al-Qaeda and the Road to 9/11*. New York: Knopf, 2006.

Index

About the Author

Historian and award-winning author Don Nardo has written many books for young people about events connected to the Middle East and terrorism. In addition, he is a specialist in ancient history. Nardo, who also composes and arranges orchestral music, lives with his wife, Christine, in Massachusetts.